Smithsonian

SOLAR SYSTEM

Ruth Strother

CONTENTS

The Solar System

A solar system is a star and the planets, planets' moons, and other space objects that move around the star.

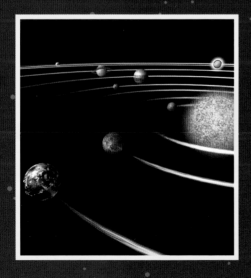

Our solar system moves around one star that we call the Sun.

There are probably billions of other solar systems in the universe!

Stars and Sun

Stars are huge
burning balls of gas.
We can see thousands of stars in the
night sky. But only one star is in our
solar system. That star is the Sun.

The Sun is made of gas and dust. The Sun is huge! It makes up more than ninety-nine percent of the mass (or stuff) in our solar system. All other space objects in our solar system were made from the stuff that didn't get pulled into the Sun when it formed.

Gravity and Orbit

Gravity causes an object to pull other objects toward it. The force of the pull depends on the object's size. The Sun is huge, so its gravity is strong. All other objects in the solar system are pulled toward the Sun.

The Sun's gravity pulls space objects into a path. The path leads them around the Sun. This path is called an orbit.

Moons are a little different.

Moons orbit a planet. So a moon orbits its planet while the planet orbits the Sun.

Galaxy

The solar system is one small part of a galaxy. Galaxies are made of dust, gas, and billions of stars. Billions of galaxies spin in outer space. Some galaxies gather in a huge group like stars gather into galaxies.

Our galaxy has hundreds of billions of stars! From Earth, all those stars look a bit like a path of spilled milk. Our galaxy is called the Milky Way.

Mercury

Mercury

Mercury is the closest planet to the Sun.
Mercury is hard for us to see.
It is hidden by the Sun's glare.
Mercury has a thin **atmosphere**.
There is very little air or other gases
on Mercury. The sky is always black.

Mercury is a dry, rocky planet. It has huge cliffs and holes called **craters**. Mercury is freezing cold at night. But in the day, Mercury is very hot.

A day on Mercury lasts more than fifty-eight days on Earth.

Venus

Venus is the second planet from the Sun. And Venus is the closest planet to Earth. Venus and Earth are about the same size. Some people call them sisters or twins.

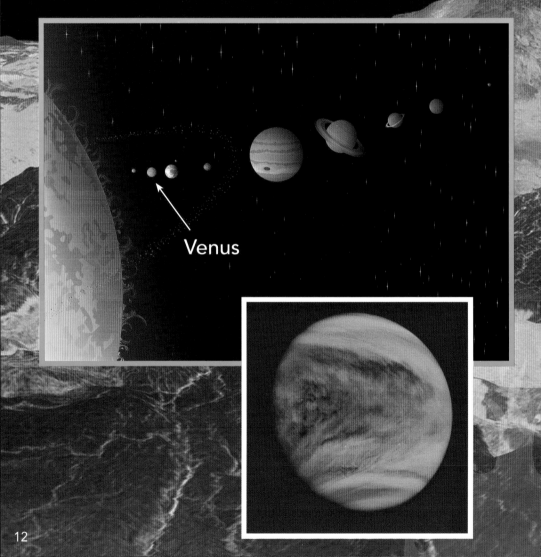

Venus

It is scorching hot on Venus. The air is full of deadly acid. The sky is yellow with strange clouds and lightning.

A day on Venus lasts more than two hundred days on Earth.

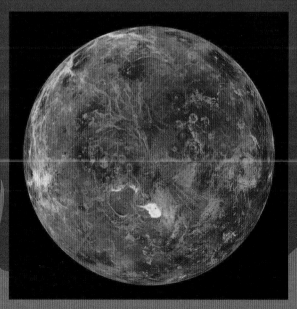

Earth

Earth

Earth is the third planet from the Sun. Earth is the only planet with liquid water on its surface. Most of Earth's surface is covered with water. It even looks blue when seen from space!

Earth has the right mix of air, water, and warmth from the Sun. This mix makes life possible. Earth is home to more than thirty million different forms of life.

Mars

Mars

Mars is the fourth planet from the Sun.
Its soil is filled with iron. The iron rusts
because of the Martian air. The rust
makes the soil look red. The red color
gives Mars its nickname, the Red Planet.

Mars may have once looked more like Earth. It even has water deep in the ground. People want to explore Mars to understand how the planet changed.

A day on Mars lasts almost as long as a day on Earth.

Jupiter

Jupiter is the fifth planet from the Sun. It is one of the gas giants. Jupiter is the biggest planet in the solar system. And Jupiter has the most moons. So far, **scientists** have found sixty-seven moons orbiting Jupiter.

Jupiter

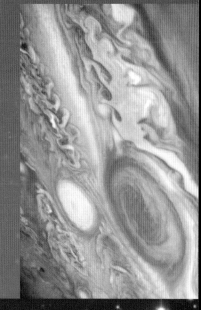

A huge storm has been whirling on Jupiter for hundreds of years. The storm is called the Great Red Spot. The Great Red Spot is as big as Earth. It used to be even bigger!

A day on Jupiter lasts about ten hours.

Saturn

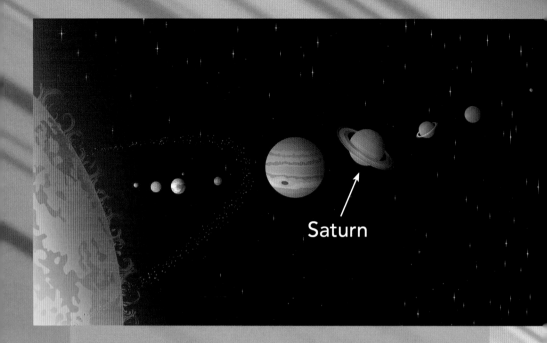

Saturn

Saturn is the sixth planet from the Sun. Saturn is famous for its seven beautiful rings. The rings are made of ice, dust, and billions of rock pieces. Some pieces are the size of tiny icy grains. Some pieces are as big as mountains!

Something strange happens about every fourteen years. Saturn's rings seem to disappear. That's because Saturn becomes tilted. When the rings' edges face Earth, we can't see them.

A day on Saturn lasts just over ten hours.

Uranus

Uranus is the seventh planet from the Sun. You need a **telescope** to see Uranus. Uranus looks like a green pea through a telescope. The green color comes from the gas in Uranus's atmosphere.

Uranus

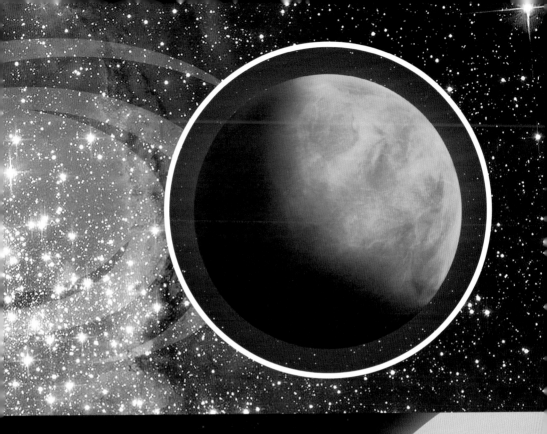

Uranus is a gas giant. Some
of the gas that covers
Uranus is icy. So Uranus
is also called the ice
giant. Uranus is the
coldest planet in our
solar system.

A day on Uranus
lasts almost
eighteen hours.

Neptune

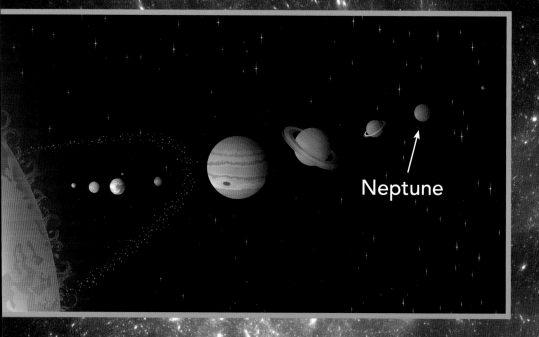

Neptune

Neptune is the eighth planet from the Sun. It has huge storms and very strong winds. Neptune is an ice giant like Uranus. But Neptune has slushy hot ice. The atmosphere on Neptune is very heavy. The heavy **pressure** keeps ice from melting.

The pressure is even heavier deep inside Neptune. Some scientists think the gas deep inside is being squeezed into diamonds!

A day on Neptune lasts about sixteen hours.

Moons

Moons are space objects. Each moon orbits a planet. The planet's gravity keeps a moon on its path.

Some planets have many moons. Some planets have no moon at all.

Jupiter has more moons than any other planet. Jupiter has sixty-seven moons.

Earth has one moon. We on Earth see just one side of the Moon. Only **astronauts** in space have seen the other side of the Moon.

Asteroids, Comets, and Meteoroids

Asteroids are large rocks that orbit the Sun. Comets orbit the Sun too. Comets are like dirty snowballs in space. They are dust and rocks trapped in frozen liquid. Meteoroids are made of rocks and metals.

Sometimes meteoroids enter Earth's atmosphere. They heat up and glow. Then they are called meteors. When you wish upon a falling star, you're wishing upon a meteor!

If the meteor hits Earth, it's called a meteorite. Some meteorites leave craters.

SOLAR SYSTEM QUIZ

1. How many stars are in our solar system?
   a) Billions and billions
   b) Thousands
   c) One

2. What do moons orbit?
   a) The Sun
   b) A planet
   c) The Solar System

3. Which planet is sometimes called Earth's sister or twin?
   a) Venus
   b) Mars
   c) Mercury

4. Which planet has more moons than any other planet?

a) Saturn

b) Uranus

c) Jupiter

5. What is the Great Red Spot?

a) A huge storm

b) A massive crater

c) A giant cloud

6. What are Saturn's rings made of?

a) Gases and colorful clouds

b) Comets and asteroids

c) Ice, dust, and rock pieces

GLOSSARY

Astronauts: people who are trained to travel into outer space

Atmosphere: the gases surrounding a planet or moon

Craters: large dents on the surface of a planet or moon made by a meteorite

Pressure: the ongoing force from one object pushing or pressing against another object

Scientists: people who are experts in science

Telescope: a tool that makes distant objects look closer and bigger